Score
with
Baseball Math

Stuart A. P. Murray

Enslow Elementary
an imprint of
Enslow Publishers, Inc.
40 Industrial Road
Box 398
Berkeley Heights, NJ 07922
USA

http://www.enslow.com

Enslow Elementary, an imprint of Enslow Publishers, Inc.
Enslow Elementary® is a registered trademark of Enslow Publishers, Inc.

Library of Congress Cataloging-in-Publication Data

Murray, Stuart, 1948-
  Score with baseball math / Stuart A. P. Murray.
     pages cm. — (Score with sports math)
  Includes index.
  Summary: "Get fun baseball facts while practicing math techniques used in baseball such as figuring
out batting averages. Also includes math problem-solving tips"—Provided by publisher.
  ISBN 978-0-7660-4174-5
  1. Baseball—Mathematics--Juvenile literature. I. Title.
  GV867.5.M87 2014
  796.357—dc23

                                                       2012028797

Future editions:
Paperback ISBN: 978-1-4644-0287-6
Single-User PDF ISBN: 978-1-4646-1180-3

EPUB ISBN: 978-1-4645-1180-6
Multi-User PDF ISBN: 978-0-7660-5809-5

Printed in China
012013 Leo Paper Group, Heshan City, Guangdong, China
10 9 8 7 6 5 4 3 2 1

To Our Readers: We have done our best to make sure all Internet Addresses in this book were
active and appropriate when we went to press. However, the author and the publisher have no
control over and assume no liability for the material available on those Internet sites or on other Web
sites they may link to. Any comments or suggestions can be sent by e-mail to comments@enslow.com
or to the address on the back cover.

Design and production: Rachel Turetsky, Lily Book Productions

Illustration Credits: Alan C. Heison/Shutterstock.com, p. 33; Anthony Correia/Shutterstock.com,
p. 27; Aspen Photo/Shutterstock.com, pp. 6, 8, 12, 38, 44; Brad Collett/Shutterstock.com, p. 13;
© 2012 Clipart.com, pp. 3, 5 (top and bottom), 9, 16, 17, 19, 21, 29, 30, 31, 35, 39; Daniel M.
Silva/Shutterstock.com, p. 14; Debby Wong/Shutterstock.com, p. 22; doodle/Shutterstock.com,
pp. 25, 41, 46; Eric Broder Van Dyke/Shutterstock.com, pp. 4, 7; Eugene Buchko/Shutterstock.
com, p. 36; Glen Jones/Shutterstock.com, p. 10 (bottom); Haessly Photography/Shutterstock, p. 42;
Israel Pabon/Shutterstock.com, p. 28; iStockphoto.com/Stephanie Horrocks, p. 37; iStockphoto.
com/Talaj, p. 11; Jamie Roach/Shutterstock, p. 45; Library of Congress Prints and Photographs
Division Washington, D.C., p. 10 (top); Nagel Photography/Shutterstock, p. 43; Stephen McSweeny/
Shutterstock, p. 18; Thomas M. Spindle/Shutterstock.com, p. 40; Todd Taulman/Shutterstock.
com, p. 1; Wikimedia/*Baseball Digest*, p. 24; Wikimedia/Dave Hogg, p. 15; Wikimedia/Ewen and
Donabe, p. 23; Wikimedia/Jauerback, p. 32; Wikimedia/SD Dirk, p. 20.

Cover Photo: Shutterstock.com

Contents

The Yankees' Derek Jeter bats against the Oakland A's in Oakland in 2010.

INTRODUCTION
Baseball:
The All-American Game

During baseball season, ballparks and stadiums echo with the crack of bats and the roar of the crowd. You may already know about baseball and its many numbers: 9 players on the field, 9 innings in a game, 60 feet 6 inches from home plate to the mound, 3 strikes and you're out. But do you know how much math there really is in baseball? In this book, you'll learn some baseball facts and history, and you'll practice math, too. Knowing math makes playing or watching baseball even more exciting.

Baseball math is more than fun

Baseball players use math to find out their own statistics (stats). And stats tell how good players are: How many hits do they have? How many strikeouts? How many errors?

Baseball math also can be a challenge. As you'll learn in this book, some baseball math problems have several parts.

For instance, figuring a batting average isn't just counting the number of hits in a certain number of at bats. You have to do some subtraction first, and then some division.

Of course, the easiest baseball math can be the most awesome: comparing "tape measure" home runs and who hit the most of them.

This long fly ball did not measure up. It is caught at the wall by Cardinals outfielder Ryan Ludwick.

Baseball math also involves shapes, dimensions, and geometry. The infield is a diamond with four equal sides—really a square. There are even rules about the bat's dimensions: its length, thickness, and weight.

Baseball math has lots of measurements. There are 90 feet from base to base. How far does a home run ball fly to get over the left field fence?

Stars, stats, and the World Series

Baseball has been a highlight of American life and sports since the 1800s. Season after season, the fans come out to see their favorite players. They have cheered for great home-run hitters like Babe Ruth, Roger Maris, and Hank Aaron.

Fans study the stats of star pitchers like Sandy Koufax, Greg Maddux, and Mariano Rivera. The top ballplayers usually get a chance to play in the World Series sometime in their careers. The Series is baseball's most thrilling event.

Fans in San Francisco's AT&T Park watch the 2010 World Series between the San Francisco Giants and the Texas Rangers.

1

Batter Up!
Home Runs and Batting Averages

Baseball is called "a game of inches." The speedy base runner beats the throw to first by an inch. The umpire calls "Ball four!" on a curve that just misses the plate. And a blast that looks like a game-winning homer lands inches foul.

Baseball is also a game of numbers, especially when it comes to batting. Hitters keep close track of their batting averages. Baseball is also a game of homers. Batters who hit the most home runs are baseball's superstars.

National League all-star Ryan Howard hits a home run for his team, the Philadelphia Phillies.

Sluggers: "the Babe" to "Slammin' Sammy"

This table lists players by the number of home runs they hit in a season. Barry Bonds of the Giants is first, with 73 homers in 2001. Three players hold more than one place in the top 10: Ruth (1921, 1927), McGwire (1997, 1998, 1999), and Sosa (1998, 1999, 2001). Four players share 10th place with 58 homers.

This photo shows Babe Ruth in 1920, the year he joined the Yankees.

Top Home Run Hitters

	Player	Home Runs	Year
1st	Barry Bonds	73	2001
2nd	Mark McGwire	70	1998
3rd	Sammy Sosa	66	1998
4th	Mark McGwire	65	1999
5th	Sammy Sosa	64	2001
6th	Sammy Sosa	63	1999
7th	Roger Maris	61	1961
8th	Babe Ruth	60	1927
9th	Babe Ruth	59	1921
10th	Jimmie Foxx	58	1932
	Hank Greenberg	58	1938
	Ryan Howard	58	2006
	Mark McGwire	58	1997

The table shows that for most of the last one hundred years, two players held the season home run record: Babe Ruth and Roger Maris, both of the Yankees. Ruth's 1927 record of 60 homers lasted until 1961. Maris broke Ruth's record that year, with 61 homers.

Q: How many years did Ruth's record last before Maris broke it?

A: Subtract 1927 from 1961:
$1961 - 1927 = 34$ years

MATH TEST
100%

OUT
OF THE
PARK!

Q: Mark McGwire is listed more than once for homers in a season. How many total homers did he hit in those seasons?

A: McGwire is listed three times for the most home runs in a season:
58 (1997), 70 (1998), and 65 (1999)
$58 + 70 + 65 = 193$ homers

Sammy Sosa bats for the Orioles in 2005, near the end of his career.
Sosa hit 609 home runs during his 19 Major League Baseball seasons.

Maris's record was broken by two players in the
same year, 1998: Mark McGwire of the Cardinals,
with 70 homers, and Sammy Sosa of the Cubs,
with 66.

Q: How many years did Maris's record last?
A: McGwire and Sosa both broke Maris's 1961
   record in 1998. Subtract 1961 from 1998:
   1998 − 1961 = 37 years

The all-time leader for homers in a season is Barry
Bonds of the Giants, who hit 73 in 2001. This was
just three years after McGwire's 1998 record.

Q: How many more homers did Bonds hit in 2001 than Ruth hit in 1927?

A: Subtract Ruth's 60 homers from Bonds's 73:

$73 - 60 = 13$

Bonds had 13 more homers.

A home run hitter's skill is seen by comparing the number of home runs with his total at bats. The fewer at bats a hitter has, the harder it is to get the most homers. Compare the number of homers and at bats these record holders had.

Ruth	60 homers in 540 at bats
Maris	61 homers in 590 at bats
McGwire	70 homers in 509 at bats
Sosa	66 homers in 643 at bats
Bonds	73 homers in 476 at bats

Q: Which player hit the most homers with the fewest at bats?

A: Bonds had the most homers, 73, but the fewest at bats, 476. That makes his record even more impressive!

Barry Bonds of the Giants hits career home run number 723 in 2006. He retired in 2007, leading the MLB with 762 career home runs.

Q: They called Sosa "Slammin' Sammy" for his 609 homers. He had the most at bats of the listed record holders. How many more at bats did he have than Bonds (476)?

A: Subtract Bonds's 476 at bats from Sosa's 643:

643 − 476 = 167

Sosa had 167 more at bats than Bonds.

A baseball bat has to meet strict rules about size and thickness. Bats may be no more than 42 inches long. They may weigh no more than 33 ounces.

The barrel is the thickest part. It may be no more than 2¾ inches in diameter. The bat handle is much thinner than the barrel. At the bottom of the bat handle is the knob.

Q: The barrel of a bat is 2½ inches in diameter, and the knob is ½ of that diameter. What is the diameter of the knob?

A: Divide 2½ inches by 2.
$$2 \div 2 = 1, \text{ and } \frac{1}{2} \div 2 = \frac{1}{4}$$
The knob is 1¼ inches in diameter.

Q: Write the record homers hit by the bats at right as ordinal numbers.

A: Sixtieth, sixty-first, seventieth, sixty-sixth.

Bats that hit the record home runs: (l–r) Babe Ruth (60, 1927); Roger Maris (61, 1961); Mark McGwire (70, 1998); Sammy Sosa (66, 1998).

The "bat drop" and batting averages

When choosing a bat, players figure out the "bat drop." This is the bat's weight minus its length. For instance, a 33-ounce bat that's 30 inches long would have a drop of 3, since 33 − 30 = 3.

Larger drops increase the speed of the swing. Smaller drops give more power.

MORE SPEED!

Q: One bat is 29 inches long and weighs 31 ounces. A second bat is 28 inches and 33 ounces. Which bat gives a faster swing?

A: Find the drop of the first: 31 − 29 = 2
Then the second: 33 − 28 = 5
The second bat has the larger drop, so it has the faster swing.

The batting average is one of the most important statistics in baseball. It is the number of hits divided by the player's at bats. To find out a player's at bats, some batting results are subtracted from the times he came to the plate. These include walks, hit by a pitch, and bases reached on fielding errors.

$$\frac{\text{15 walks} + \text{3 hit by a pitch} + \text{7 fielding errors}}{\text{No at bats}}$$

Q: A player came to the plate 121 times. He walked 15 times, was hit by pitches 3 times, and reached on errors 7 times. How many at-bats did he have?

A: Add walks, hit by pitches, and bases on errors.

15 + 3 + 7 = 25

Subtract the total from his 121 times at the plate.

121 − 25 = 96 at bats

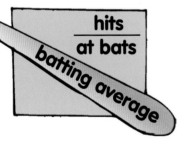

$$\frac{\text{hits}}{\text{at bats}}$$

batting average

A player's batting average is found by dividing hits by at bats. This is a decimal number shown to three places after the decimal.

Q: The ballplayer had 30 hits in his 96 at bats. Estimate his batting average to the nearest thousandth.

A: Divide 96 into 30:

30 ÷ 96 = .3125

Round .3125 to the nearest thousandth: .313

2

Pitching, Catching, and the World Series

The pitcher and the catcher are a team. In few other sports do two teammates have to work so closely together.

The pitcher needs good control for the team to win. But the catcher helps the pitcher strike out batters. The catcher signals to the pitcher what kind of pitch to throw: a fastball, a curve, or a slider low and away.

A pitching ace makes the catcher's job easier. As long as the umpire is calling strikes, of course.

The Arizona Diamondbacks' 6 ft 10 in starting pitcher Randy Johnson, nicknamed "The Big Unit," throws a strike.

Starters, relievers, and no-hitters

Baseball teams have top pitchers who take turns "starting" games. When starters tire, they are replaced by "relief" pitchers. A team throws 120 to 170 pitches per game.

Q: An ace starter throws 107 pitches in 6 innings before being relieved. The reliever throws another 55 pitches in 3 innings. What is the average number of pitches per inning?

A: Add the pitchers' totals to find the game total:

107 + 55 = 162 pitches

Divide the total pitches (162) by the game's 9 innings:

162 ÷ 9 = 18 pitches per inning

Q: The starting pitcher allows 4 runs, and the reliever allows 3 runs. Whose average runs per inning is higher?

A: Divide each pitcher's runs by the number of innings he pitched and round off to the nearest hundredth:

Starter: 4 ÷ 6 = .67 average runs per inning

Reliever: 3 ÷ 3 = 1 average run per inning

The reliever's average runs per inning (1) is higher than the starter's (.67).

Runs ÷ Innings = Average Runs Per Inning

A "shutout" is when a team allows no runs. A "no-hitter" is when it allows no hits. A "perfect game" is when no runners get on base. In 1956, Yankee great Don Larsen pitched the only perfect game there has ever been at the World Series.

Q: Larsen threw 97 pitches to beat the Dodgers.
   How many pitches did he average per batter?
A: Multiply 3 Dodger batters per inning times
   9 innings: 3 x 9 = 27 batters
   Divide total pitches (97) by total batters (27)
   and round off to the nearest tenth.
   97 ÷ 27 = 3.59, which rounds off to 3.6 pitches

New York Met Johan Santana
throws during spring training.

There were 274 no-hitters from 1875 to 2012. On June 1, 2012, Johan Santana threw number 275. It was the first one ever for the New York Mets.

Q: Find the average number of
   no-hitters per season since 1875.
   Round to the nearest hundredth.
A: To find the number of seasons,
   subtract 1875 from 2012:
   2012 − 1875 = 137 seasons
Divide 275 no-hitters by 137 seasons:
275 ÷ 137 = 2.007, which rounds off to 2.01
no-hitters

Leading Cy Young Winners

Pitcher	Won	Years
Roger Clemens	7	1986, 1987, 1991, 1997, 1998, 2001, 2004
Randy Johnson	5	1995, 1999, 2000, 2001, 2002
Steve Carlton	4	1972, 1977, 1980, 1982
Greg Maddux	4	1992, 1993, 1994, 1995
Sandy Koufax	3	1963, 1965, 1966
Pedro Martinez	3	1997, 1999, 2000
Jim Palmer	3	1973, 1975, 1976
Tom Seaver	3	1969, 1973, 1975

This table lists the pitchers who have won the most Cy Young Awards.

Best pitcher's award

The Cy Young Award is given each year to the best pitcher in the American and National Leagues. It is named for pitcher Cy Young.

Q: Who won it the most years in a row?

A: Two pitchers: Johnson: 1999, 2000, 2001, and 2002; and Maddux: 1992, 1993, 1994, and 1995.

Q: Which pitcher was first to win the award?

A: Sandy Koufax, in 1963.

Yankee catcher
Elston Howard tries
to tag out a Cincinnati
player in the 1961
World Series.

A World Series star

Yankee Elston Howard played in 9 Series from
1955–64. He also played in 1 series for the Red
Sox, a 1967 loss. And he was a Yankee coach
for 2 Series wins (1977 and 1978).

Q: How many World Series were Howard's
   teams in?

A: Add 9 as a Yankee player + 1 as a Red Sox player
   + 2 as a coach:
   9 + 1 + 2 = 12 Series

As a player, Howard was in 6 Series losses,
which is an MLB record.

Q: Of the 9 Series as a Yankee player, how many wins did Howard have?

A: Subtract the Red Sox loss from the 6 total losses: $6 - 1 = 5$

Subtract 5 losses from the 9 total Yankee Series: $9 - 5 = 4$ Series won as a player

Attempted steal

The pitcher begins the pitch. The runner on first takes off to steal. The catcher receives the pitch and rifles the ball to the second baseman. The runner's out! The whole play lasted 4.5 seconds.

Q: The catcher's throw got to second base in 1 second. How long before the catcher got it off?

A: Subtract 1 second from 4.5 seconds.

$4.5 - 1 = 3.5$ seconds from the pitch to the throw

Q: What geometric shapes are formed by the line of the throw and the diamond?

A: Two triangles. The base lines form two sides. The catcher's throw is the third side of both triangles.

Teams With the Most World Series Wins

Team	Series Wins	Series Played	Last Won
New York Yankees	27	40	2009
St. Louis Cardinals	11	18	2011
Oakland Athletics	9	14	1989
Boston Red Sox	7	11	2007
San Francisco Giants	6	18	2010
Los Angeles Dodgers	6	18	1988

The New York Yankees have won more World Series than any other team.

Q: Which teams' wins, when added together, equal the Yankees' 27 wins?

A: St. Louis (11), Oakland (9), and Boston (7)

$$11 + 9 + 7 = 27$$

Q: Which team won exactly ⅓ of the Series it played in?

A: Both the Giants and the Dodgers won 6 out of 18 Series they played in.

Make a fraction of wins to series appearances: $\frac{6}{18}$

Reduce by dividing the numerator and denominator by 6. The resulting fraction is ⅓.

Q: Which teams won more than half of the Series they played in?

A: The Yankees, Cardinals, Athletics, and Red Sox all won more than half the Series they played in. Multiply each team's wins by 2 and compare the product with the number of Series they played in.

Q: Is there another way to figure out which teams won more than half the Series they played in?

A: Yes. Divide the number of Series played by 2 and compare the quotient to the number won. For example, Boston's 11 Series played divided by 2 = 5½; Boston won 7 World Series, which is more than 5½.

Star pitcher Mariano Rivera was key to many Series wins for the Yankees.

3

The Ballpark:
Home Plate
to Deep Center

Every baseball stadium has its own personality. Some, like Boston's 100-year-old Fenway Park, are rich in baseball history. Miami's modern Marlins Park, built in 2012, has a roof that can be closed to keep out rain.

There are several designs used for baseball parks. These include jewel box (classic parks), multipurpose parks for other events, and indoor stadiums.

Whatever the design, the playing fields (or "ball fields") have the same parts: the infield diamond and the outfield.

The Red Sox play a night game at Boston's Fenway Park. Built in 1912, it is Major League Baseball's oldest.

This 1866 ballpark was in Hoboken, New Jersey. Baseball was just getting started.

Playing fields

Baseball was first played in parks or fields. There were few home runs because there was no outfield fence to hit over.

Q: An old-time "batsman" slugs a ball far into left field and it keeps on rolling. He runs with an average speed of 5 seconds base-to-base. How long does it take him to reach home?

A: He touches 3 bases plus home:

4 bases × 5 seconds = 20 seconds for a home run

No matter what ballpark they are in, infielders play on the same size diamond every game. The bases are always 90 ft apart. The distance from third base to first base is about 127 ft. The depth of the infield is measured from home plate to the grass line: about 127 ft. The depth of center field is usually twice the depth of the infield plus 25 ft.

Q: **What is the approximate depth of the outfield?**
A: **Multiply 127 ft × 2 = 254 ft**
   Then add another 25 ft.
   254 ft + 25 ft = 279 ft

Q: **What is the approximate distance from home to the farthest part of the outfield fence?**
A: **Add to 279 ft the 127 ft of the infield depth:**
   279 ft + 127 ft = 406 ft

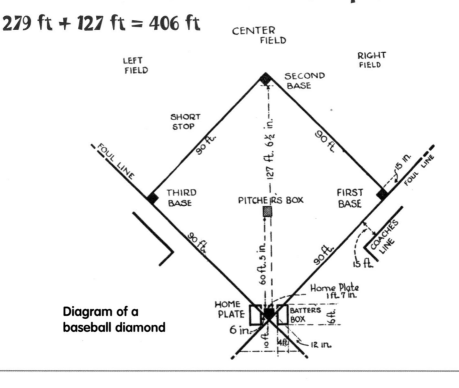

Diagram of a baseball diamond

The high roof makes Wrigley Field's grandstand look like a giant jewel box with the lid open. This is a jewel box design.

Grandstands and lights

Stadiums were built after many spectators began coming to games. The oldest ballparks still in use are Boston's Fenway Park (1912) and Chicago's Wrigley Field (1914). Both are jewel box parks.

Q: A decade is 10 years. How many decades were there between the opening of Fenway Park, built in 1912 and Miami's Marlins Park, built in 2012?

A: Subtract 1912 from 2012:
2012 − 1912 = 100 years
Divide 100 years by 10 years:
100 ÷ 10 = 10 decades

Fenway installed lights for night games in 1946. Wrigley was the last ballpark to get lights, in 1988.

Q: How many years after Fenway did Wrigley get lights?

A: Subtract 1946 from 1988.

1988 – 1946= 42 years

Q: A third baseman snags a line drive going 180 ft per second. Third base is 90 ft from home. How much time did he have after the ball was hit?

A: Divide speed per second (180 ft) into the distance (90 ft):

90 ÷ 180 = .5 , or ½

The third baseman had half a second to catch the ball.

Seattle Mariners third baseman Adrián Beltré makes the play. Third is the "hot corner" because balls are hit so hard.

The most seating and biggest outfields

Outfielders roam the wide open spaces to haul in long drives or get under high fly balls. And some of those spaces are much bigger than others, as seen in the table below.

The Largest Ballparks

Stadium	Team	Seating	LF	CF	RF
Dodger Stadium	Dodgers	56,000	330'	400'	330'
Yankee Stadium	Yankees	52,325	318'	408'	314'
Coors Field	Rockies	50,445	347'	415'	350'
Turner Field	Braves	50,096	335'	400'	330'
Rogers Centre	Blue Jays	49,539	328'	400'	328'
Rangers Ballpark	Rangers	49,115	330'	400'	330'
Chase Field	Diamondbacks	49,033	330'	407'	335'
Oriole Park	Orioles	48,876	333'	410'	318'

This table gives seating capacity and shows the distance in feet from home plate to deep center and to the foul poles in left field and right field.

Q: Which ballpark in the table has the longest distances to its fences?

A: Coors Field has the biggest outfield: 347 ft to left, 415 ft to center, and 350 ft to right.

A home run ball flies over the Orioles center field fence. It lands five rows up in the stands. Each row counts for 5 feet in the distance the ball travels.

Q: What is the total distance the ball traveled?

A: Multiply 5 (rows of seats) × 5 ft = 25 ft. Then check the table for the distance to the Orioles center field (CF) fence. Add the numbers: 410 ft + 25 ft = 435 ft

Foul poles are at the ends of the foul lines and in fair territory. If a ball hits the pole, it's a home run.

Q: Which ballpark in the table has the shortest distance to a foul pole?

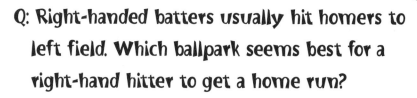

A: Yankee Stadium: 314 ft to the right field foul pole.

Q: Right-handed batters usually hit homers to left field. Which ballpark seems best for a right-hand hitter to get a home run?

A: Also Yankee Stadium, with the shortest distance to the left field foul pole: 318 ft.

It's a record crowd and a perfect summer evening at Atlanta's Turner Field.

"Buy me peanuts and Cracker Jacks!"

A big game had a crowd of 50,125. One-tenth of the fans sat in the bleachers. The other nine-tenths were in the grandstand.

Q: Estimate to the nearest thousand: How many fans were in the bleachers? In the grandstand?

A: Round off the crowd to 50,000. Then divide by 10 to find how many were in the bleachers.

50,000 ÷ 10 = 5,000 in the bleachers

Subtract that number from 50,000.

50,000 − 5,000 = 45,000 in the grandstand

Fans can buy more refreshments than peanuts and Cracker Jacks. You've saved $2 a week for 10 weeks just to spend at the game.

Q: In one stadium a cold drink costs $5 and a hot dog costs $7. In another stadium they cost $5.75 and $8. Which stadium has the better deal?

A: Add the price of hot dogs and cold drinks at each stadium.

First: $5 + $7 = $12

Second: $5.75 + $8 = $13.75

The first stadium has the better deal.

Q: In which stadium could you afford 1 drink and 2 hot dogs?

A: Add on the price of a second hot dog:

First: $12 + $7 = $19

Second: $13.75 + $8 = $21.75

Find out your savings. Multiply 10 weeks by $2

$10 \times \$2 = \$20$

Compare your $20 to the cost at each stadium. You could afford 1 drink and 2 hot dogs only at the first stadium.

4

Championship Series:

Sluggers vs. Cannons

The Centerville Sluggers visit the Duketown Cannons for the league's championship series.

The old song "Take Me Out to the Ball Game" tells us to "root, root, root for the home team, if they don't win, it's a shame!" Well, the Cannons are the home team, and they soon take the lead. But the Sluggers won't give up.

Follow the game and do the math as the visiting team battles back.

A shortstop tries to keep this runner from stealing second base.

A batter prepares to attempt a bunt.

The big seventh game

The Centerville Sluggers come to bat against the Duketown Cannons. It's the seventh and final game of their championship series. The series is tied.

Q: How many games has each team won?

A: The 2 teams have played 6 games with an equal number of wins.

Divide 6 (games) by 2 (teams):

6 ÷ 2 = 3 games each

In the first inning, a Slugger gets on with a bunt. Then, Slugger star Miguel Cross homers. But the Cannons score 2 in the second and 2 in the third.

Q: How many runs does each team have?

A: The Sluggers have 2 runs. The Cannons scored twice in two innings: 2 + 2 = 4 runs.

Runs on the scoreboard are shown with the visitors at top, home at bottom.

Q: How does the scoreboard show the score of the game?

A: The visiting Sluggers at top, and the Cannons at bottom: 2–4.

The pitchers don't allow any more runs. The score stays 2–4 until the ninth inning.

Q: How many runs do the Sluggers have to score to take the lead?

A: The Sluggers need 5 runs total. Subtract 2 from 5.

5 – 2 = 3 runs to take the lead

This batter swings with power for the fence.

The ninth inning

It's the top of the ninth. Two Sluggers get on base. Then Miguel Cross hits another home run.

Q: What's the score now?
A: The homer scored 3 runs.
The Sluggers already had 2, so:
3 + 2 = 5. They're leading, 5–4.

Miguel had 14 hits in 24 at bats in the first 6 games. In the seventh he gets 2 more in 4 at bats.

Q: What is Miguel's batting average for the series?
A: Add Miguel's 14 hits to 2 in the seventh game:
14 + 2 = 16 hits
Add 24 at bats to 4 at bats in the seventh game:
24 + 4 = 28
Divide total hits (16) by total at bats (28):
16 ÷ 28 = .5714
Round to the nearest thousandth:
.5714 = .571 batting average

The Sluggers don't score any more runs. Now the Cannons come to bat. Sluggers pitcher, Johnny "the Jet" Cohen, is tired. He has thrown 100 pitches in the first 8 innings.

Q: How many pitches is "the Jet" averaging per inning?

A: Divide 100 pitches by 8 innings.

100 ÷ 8 = 12.5 pitches per inning.

The pitcher winds up, ready to show his best stuff.

The first Cannon strikes out. Then Bobby Downs doubles. Next, he steals third. Bobby has 4 stolen bases in 7 attempts in the series.

Q: What's Bobby's stealing percentage?

A: Divide 4 stolen bases by 7 attempts:

$4 \div 7 = .5714$

Round to the nearest hundredth: $.5714 = .57$

Multiply by 100 to convert to a percentage:

$.57 \times 100 = 57\%$

The batter swings and drives the ball for extra bases.

The next batter walks. Davey Blake is up. If he drives Bobby home, it ties the game, 5–5. Davey has 2 hits in 3 at bats.

Q: As a fraction, what is Davey's batting average for this game?

A: The 2 hits are the numerator and 3 at bats the denominator. Davey's batting average as a fraction is ⅔.

Davey hits a grounder up the middle. Bobby starts for home. The shortstop gets the ball at second and tags the base. Runner out! He then throws to first! Double play!

Q: How far did the ball travel? (Home to second is about 127 ft, second to first is 90 ft.)

A: The ball was batted from home to second, then thrown from second to first: 127 ft + 90 ft = 217 ft (minus the first baseman's stretch!)

The Centerville Sluggers win, 5–4!

Out number three! The winning team celebrates a championship.

Math Problem-Solving Tips

✏️ Always read the problem completely before beginning to work on it.

✏️ Make sure you understand the question.

✏️ Some problems require more than one step to find the final answer.

✏️ Don't think you always have to use every number in the problem. Some numbers are extra information and are not needed for the calculations.

✏️ If you know your answer is wrong but can't find the mistake, then start again on a clean sheet of paper.

✏️ Don't get upset! You can solve problems better when you're calm.

✏️ If you're stuck on a problem, go on with the rest of them. You can come back to it.

Further Reading

Books

Connolly, Sean. *The Book of Perfectly Perilous Math: 24 Death-Defying Challenges for Young Mathematicians.* New York: Workman Publishing Company, 2012.

Fitzgerald, Theresa. *Math Dictionary for Kids: The Essential Guide to Math Terms, Strategies, and Tables.* Waco, Tex.: Prufrock Press, Inc., 2011.

The Complete Book of Math, Grades 3–4. Greensboro, N.C.: American Education Publishing, 2009.

Web Sites

Basic Mathematics. 2008.
<basic-mathematics.com/calculate-baseball-statistics.html>
This web site offers an understanding of mathematical concepts and operations. This section shows the relationship between math and baseball.

Doina Popovici. Math-Play.com. 2010.
<math-play.com/baseball-math.html>
This site's free online math games are among a variety of games for elementary and middle grades. They are organized by grade level, content, and game type.

Index